The Only
SUGAR FREE CAKES & BAKES
Recipes You'll Ever Need

The Cake & Bake Academy

First published in 2015 by Kyle Craig Publishing

Text and illustration copyright © 2015 Kyle Craig Publishing

Editor: Alison McNicol

Design: Julie Anson

With thanks to Frances Williams

ISBN: 978-1-908707-65-9

A CIP record for this book is available from the British Library.

A Kyle Craig Publication

www.kyle-craig.com

Contents

CHOCOLATE CAKE WITH GANACHE

Ingredients

Cake:
180g/ 6 oz almond flour
150g/ 5½ oz cocoa powder
260g/ 9½ oz pitted dates
½ tsp baking soda
3 medium eggs
120ml/ 4 fl oz water
2 tbsp coconut oil
2 tsp vanilla essence
Pinch salt

Chocolate Ganache topping:
25g/ 1 oz unsweetened cocoa powder
75ml/ 3 fl oz heavy/double cream
½ tsp vanilla essence
1 tbsp powdered Stevia

Method

Preheat the oven to 170C / 325F / Gas Mark 3

Mix together the cocoa powder, almond flour, baking soda and salt in a bowl.

Place the dates and water in a food processor and blend until it forms a smooth paste.

Mix the date paste with the eggs, coconut oil, vanilla essence and mix until smooth.

Combine all the ingredients together and stir until smooth.

Pour into a greased 20cm/ 8" round cake pan.

Bake for 25-30 minutes, or until a toothpick comes out clean. Allow to cool before adding the ganache.

Ganache:

Heat the cream, powdered Stevia and vanilla extract over low heat in a sauce pan.

Once it comes to a gentle boil turn off heat and whisk in cocoa powder until smooth. Pour over the cake and garnish to suit.

RED VELVET CAKE

Ingredients

250g/ 9 oz plain/ all-purpose flour
1 tbsp unsweetened cocoa
140g/ 5 oz Splenda (granulated)
100g/ 3 oz Trex/ vegetable shortening
250ml/ 8 fl oz buttermilk
60ml/ 2 fl oz red food colouring
2 eggs
1 tsp baking soda
1 tsp salt
1 tsp vanilla essence
1 tsp white vinegar
Vanilla Cream Cheese Frosting recipe: see p.41

Method

Preheat the oven to 180C / 350F / Gas Mark 4

In a large bowl, mix the shortening, Splenda and eggs. In another bowl mix the red food colouring and cocoa until it forms a paste, then add to the other ingredients in the large bowl.

Add the buttermilk then gradually add in the flour, beating slowly. Add baking soda, vanilla essence and vinegar and beat for 2 more mins.

Pour into two 20cm/ 8" greased cake tins. Bake for 25-30 minutes, or until a toothpick comes out clean. Allow to cool before adding the Vanilla Cream Cheese Frosting.

Next, make double the Vanilla Cream Cheese Frosting recipe from p.41.

When cakes are cooled, sandwich them together with a layer of frosting, then spread the remainder over top and sides of cake. Decorate as desired.

If you cannot find buttermilk, you can easily make your own alternative. Combine 250ml milk with one 15ml tablespoon of lemon juice or white wine vinegar. Stir well and leave to stand for 5 minutes before using.

LEMON CAKE

Ingredients

300g/ 11 oz plain/ all-purpose flour
100g/ 3½ oz butter, softened
100g/ 3½ oz mashed ripe banana
3 eggs
60ml/ 2 fl oz semi-skimmed/ reduced fat milk
4 tbsp freshly squeezed lemon juice
200g/ 7 oz Greek yoghurt
2 tsp vanilla essence
2 tsp baking powder
1 tsp baking soda

Method

Preheat the oven to 170C / 325F / Gas Mark 3

In a large mixing bowl, beat together the mashed banana, eggs and butter until smooth.

To this mixture add the Greek yoghurt, lemon juice, milk and vanilla. Beat slowly until mixed, then add all the other ingredients and beat until you have a smooth batter.

Pour into a greased loaf tin.

Bake for 25 to 30 minutes or until a toothpick inserted in centre comes out clean. Allow to cool.

VICTORIA SPONGE CAKE

Ingredients

For the sponge:
150g/ 6 oz plain/ all-purpose flour
150g/ 6 oz butter
3 eggs
150g/ 6 oz Sweetly Stevia
½ tsp vanilla essence

For the buttercream:
100g/ 4 oz Sweetly Stevia
50g/ 2 oz butter
½ tsp of vanilla essence
Jam – use your preferred sugar-free jam

Method

Preheat the oven to 170C / 325F / Gas Mark 3

Sieve the flour into a bowl and add the Sweetly Stevia, butter and vanilla essence. Add the eggs and beat well until the mixture is light and fluffy.

Pour into two greased and lined 18cm/ 7" round tins. Bake for 30 to 40 minutes or until golden brown and a toothpick comes out clean. Leave to sit for 5 minutes in the tins, then turn out to cool.

For the buttercream, sieve the Sweetly Stevia into a bowl, add the butter and vanilla essence and beat well until creamy and fluffy.

Sandwich the cakes together with a layer of your favourite sugar-free jam followed by a layer of the buttercream. Dust with powdered Stevia to finish.

BANANA WALNUT CAKE

Ingredients

250g/ 9 oz plain/ all-purpose flour
200g/ 7 oz mashed bananas
120g/ 4 oz butter, softened
125g/ 4 oz chopped walnuts
3 eggs
180ml/ 6 fl oz water
1 tsp ground cinnamon
2 tsp baking powder
1 tsp baking soda

Method

Preheat the oven to 180C / 350F / Gas Mark 4

In a large bowl beat the bananas and butter until creamy.

Add the eggs and beat well. Combine the flour, baking powder, baking soda and cinnamon and add to the banana mixture. Gradually add in the water and continue to beat. Stir in the chopped walnuts.

Spoon into a greased 23cm/ 9" square baking pan and bake for approx. 30 minutes or until a toothpick comes out clean. Allow to cool before serving. Delicious sliced and spread with butter.

CHOCOLATE BUNDT CAKE

Ingredients

300g/ 10 oz plain/ all-purpose flour

75g/ 3 oz unsweetened cocoa powder

150g/ 6 oz Splenda (granulated)

120g / 4 oz butter, softened

200ml/ 7 fl oz milk

3 large eggs

1 tsp vanilla essence

1 tsp baking powder

1 tsp baking soda

Chocolate Fudge Sauce recipe - see p.39

Method

Preheat the oven to 170C / 325F / Gas Mark 3

Beat the butter, eggs and Splenda well until light and creamy.

Sieve all the dry ingredients and fold carefully into the egg mixture.

Add the milk mixture and mix well.

Pour into one standard bundt pan and bake for approximately 25-30 minutes. Once cool, pour the Chocolate Fudge Sauce over the top.

CARROT CAKES

Ingredients

100g/ 3 ½ oz plain/ all-purpose flour
70g/ 2 ½ oz Sweetly Stevia
50g/ 2 oz chopped walnuts (optional)
15g/ ½ oz freshly-grated carrots
1 large egg
1 tbsp coconut oil, melted
¼ tsp baking soda
⅛ tsp baking powder
¼ tsp vanilla essence
¼ tsp ground cinnamon
Pinch of salt

Method

Preheat the oven to 180C / 350F / Gas Mark 4

In a medium bowl, combine the flour, cinnamon, baking soda and baking powder.

In another bowl, combine the rest of the ingredients and mix well.

Add the wet ingredients to the dry ingredients, and stir well to combine until you have a batter.

Divide the batter between 12 muffin cups and bake for 10-15 minutes, or until a toothpick comes out clean. Cool before serving.

CHOCOLATE ALMOND BROWNIES

Ingredients

200g/ 7 oz unsweetened chocolate
200g/ 7 oz pitted dates
110g / 4 oz chopped almonds
3 medium eggs
60ml/ 2 fl oz coconut oil, melted
1 tbsp vanilla essence
½ tsp baking soda

Method

Preheat the oven to 180C / 350F / Gas Mark 4

Add the chocolate and baking soda to a food processor and pulse until it is in a powdered consistency.

Add in the dates, eggs, coconut oil and vanilla and pulse until all the ingredients form a batter. Fold in the chopped nuts, then pour the batter into a 20 x 20cm/ 8" x 8" baking dish.

Bake for 25-30 minutes, then allow to cool before serving.

RED VELVET CUPCAKES

Ingredients

150g/5oz plain/ all-purpose flour
75g/ 2½ oz Splenda (granulated)
75g/ 2½ oz freshly puréed beetroot/ beets
(boiled until tender, then puréed)
250m/ 8 fl oz milk
60ml/2 fl oz coconut oil, melted
1½ tsp vanilla essence
¼ tsp salt
1½ tbsp unsweetened cocoa powder
1½ tsp baking powder
Vanilla Cream Cheese Frosting - see p.41

Method

Preheat the oven to 180C / 350F / Gas Mark 4

Mix the beetroot purée and coconut oil together until smooth, then mix in the Splenda and vanilla essence.

In a bowl, sift together the flour, cocoa powder, salt, and baking powder.

Slowly start adding in the flour mixture and milk a small amount of each at a time until you have a smooth batter.

Divide among 12 cupcake liners and bake for 20-25 minutes, or until a toothpick comes out clean.

Allow to cool before piping on the Vanilla Cream Cheese Frosting.

APPLE CINNAMON MUFFINS

Ingredients

240g/ 9 oz plain/ all-purpose flour
360ml/ 12 fl oz unsweetened applesauce
1 egg
2 tbsp vegetable oil
2 tsp cinnamon
¾ tsp nutmeg
¾ tsp baking soda
1½ tsp baking powder

Method

Preheat the oven to 190C / 375F / Gas Mark 5

Prepare your muffin tin with liners and set aside.

In a large bowl, beat together the egg, oil and applesauce. Add the flour, spices and all other dry ingredients and beat well until you have a smooth batter.

Pour mix into a lined 12 muffin tin.

Bake for approx. 18-22 minutes, or until a toothpick inserted in the centre comes out clean, then allow to cool before serving.

BLUEBERRY MUFFINS

Ingredients

120g/ 4 oz coconut flour
2 very ripe bananas, mashed
3 eggs, beaten
100g/ 3½ oz blueberries
4 tbsp coconut oil
Juice and zest of one lemon
1 tsp vanilla essence
½ tsp baking soda
Pinch of salt

Method

Preheat the oven to 200C / 400F / Gas Mark 6

Mash 2 medium bananas and mix in the eggs.

In a separate bowl, combine and sift the coconut flour and all other dry ingredients.

Add the vanilla extract, coconut oil, lemon juice and zest to the banana mix, then pour into the bowl with the dry ingredients.

Finally, fold in the blueberries. Pour mix into a lined 12 muffin tin and bake for 18- 20 minutes.

GINGER, DATE AND ALMOND MUFFINS

Ingredients

140g/ 5 oz self-raising flour*
140g/ 5 oz dates
50g/ 2 oz flaked almonds
1 egg
125m/ 4 fl oz apple juice
3 tbsp vegetable oil
¾ tsp ground ginger

Method

Preheat the oven to 200C / 400F / Gas Mark 6

Chop the dates into small pieces and add to a large bowl. Sieve the flour and ginger into this, then set aside.

In a separate bowl, beat the eggs, add all the wet ingredients then add this to the dry ingredients.

Mix thoroughly, then pour mix into a lined 12 muffin tin, sprinkle some flaked almonds onto each.

Bake for 18- 20 minutes.

Substitute self-raising flour for 140g/ 4oz all-purpose flour plus 2 tsps baking powder and a pinch of salt.

CHOCOLATE MUFFINS

Ingredients

240g/ 9 oz almond flour
25g/ 1 o z cocoa
1 medium-sized sweet potato, cooked
& mashed
2 medium eggs, beaten
80ml/ 3 fl oz coconut oil
1 tsp vanilla essence
½ tsp bicarb of soda/ baking soda
½ tsp salt

Method

Preheat the oven to 180C / 350F / Gas Mark 4

In a bowl, combine the almond flour, cocoa and other dry ingredients.

In another large bowl, mash your cooked sweet potato, add in the eggs, coconut oil and vanilla essence and mix until smooth. Add the dry ingredients to this bowl and mix together well.

Spoon the mix into a lined 12 muffin tin and bake for about 25-30 minutes, or until tooth-pick inserted comes out clean.

Allow to cool before serving.

COCONUT WHITE CHOCOLATE WHOOPIE PIES

Ingredients

For the cookies:
200g / 7 oz coconut flour
100g/ 4 oz dessicated coconut
1 ripe banana, mashed
120ml/ 4 fl oz coconut oil
2-3 tbsp date puree
2 medium eggs
½ tsp baking soda
1 tsp cinnamon
1 tsp vanilla essence
Pinch salt

For the filling:
120ml/ 4 fl oz coconut cream
150g /5 oz sugar-free white chocolate

Method

For the cookies:

Preheat the oven to 180C / 350F / Gas Mark 4

In a food processor/mixer, mix the flour, butter and date puree, then add in the eggs and vanilla Add in all the other ingredients except the coconut.

Remove from the food processor, then add the coconut to the bowl and mix in with a spoon.

Line a baking tray with baking parchment/ greaseproof paper. Drop and shape circles of the dough onto the paper, well spaced to allow for expansion.

Bake for around 10 minutes, or until they are golden but still soft. Remove from the oven and set aside to cool.

For the filling:

Heat the coconut cream gently in a saucepan until it is melted. Break up the chocolate into small pieces and add to the hot cream, stirring well until all melted together into a smooth paste.

Set aside or in the fridge for around 10 minutes to firm up. Once firm, pipe or spoon the mixture to sandwich your whoopee pies together.

CHOCOLATE PEANUT BUTTER COOKIES

Ingredients

400g / 14 oz chickpeas, cooked and well-rinsed
100g/ 4 oz peanuts
100g/ 4 oz unsweetened chocolate, chopped
100g/ 4 oz peanut butter (sugar-free)
60ml/ 2 fl oz milk or almond/soy milk
1 tsp baking powder
1 tsp vanilla essence

Method

Preheat the oven to 200C / 400F / Gas Mark 6

First, drain and wash the chickpeas well.

Next, add all the ingredients (except the chocolate and peanuts) into a food processor or mixer and mix until a smooth dough.

Add slightly more milk if needed. Remove from mixer and stir in the peanuts and chocolate chunks, mixing with your hands if needed.

Line a baking tray / cookie sheet with baking parchment/ greaseproof paper.

Drop spoonfuls of dough onto the paper, well spaced to allow for expansion.

Bake for around 15 minutes or until nicely golden.

OATMEAL COOKIES

Ingredients

60g/ 2 oz whole wheat flour
60g/ 2 oz oatmeal
120g/ 4 oz unsweetened applesauce
30ml/ 1 fl oz water
30ml/ 1 fl oz vegetable oil
1 egg
½ tsp vanilla essence
½ tsp ground cinnamon
¼ tsp ground allspice
½ tsp baking powder
¼ tsp baking soda

Method

Preheat the oven to 190C / 375F / Gas Mark 5

Combine all the ingredients together in a mixing bowl and beat well.

Line a baking tray/ cookie sheet with baking parchment/ greaseproof paper.

Drop spoonfuls of dough onto the paper, spaced to allow for expansion.

Bake for around 10-15 minutes or until nicely golden.

LEMON COOKIES

Ingredients

60g/ 2 oz plain/ all-purpose flour
30g/ 1o z Sweetly Stevia
4 tbsp butter
1 medium egg
Zest and juice of 1 lemon
½ tsp baking powder

Method

Preheat the oven to 180C / 350F / Gas Mark 4

Line a baking tray / cookie sheet with baking parchment/ greaseproof paper.

Cream the butter and Stevia together until soft. Next add the lemon juice and zest and gradually beat in the egg.

Sift together the flour and baking powder, and fold into the mixture. It will start to form a dough, so now use your hands to knead the dough.

Roll the cookie dough out thinly on a floured surface. Use a round cookie cutter to cut out cookies and place on baking tray, with room between for them to expand.

Bake for 10-15 minutes, or until lightly golden. Allow to cool before serving.

LEMON BARS

Ingredients

Crust
60g/ 2 oz sunflower seeds (finely ground)
90g / 3 oz coconut flour
2 medium eggs
2 tbsps unsalted butter
2 tbsps honey
1 tsp vanilla extract
2 tsps fresh lemon juice
½ tsp baking soda

Filling
3 tablespoons coconut flour
3 large eggs plus 1 yolk
½ cup honey
¾ cup fresh lemon juice
1 tsp lemon zest

Method

Preheat the oven to 180C / 350F / Gas Mark 4

Combine all of the crust ingredients in a food processor and pulse for 20 seconds to combine, and until it forms a dough.

Lightly grease a 23 x 23cm / 9"x9" square baking dish and pour and press the crust dough into the bottom of the dish. Prick all over with a fork.

Bake for 10 minutes, then remove and allow to cool. Keep the oven on while you prepare the filling.

For the filling, whisk all the ingredients together, ensuring there are no lumps and you have a smooth consistency.

Pour the filling onto the crust, then return to the oven for 15-20 minutes or until the center is set but slightly wobbly.

Cool on a wire rack, then refrigerate before serving.

APPLE PIE

Ingredients

Crust
240g/ 9 oz plain/ all-purpose flour
125g/ 4 oz Trex/ vegetable shortening
5 tbsp water
1 tsp salt

Filling
700g/ 1lb 9 oz sliced apples
120ml/ 4 fl oz unsweetened apple juice
2 tsp cornflour/ cornstarch
1 tsp cinnamon
1 tsp nutmeg

Method

Preheat the oven to 220C / 425F / Gas Mark 7
To make the crust:

Grease a round pie plate with butter or shortening.

Mix the flour and salt in a large bowl. Work in the shortening with your fingertips until mixture is completely blended and crumbly.

Add in the water, 1 tbsp at a time, blending it into your pastry until it forms a ball of dough. Too much water and it will become sticky, too little and the pastry will crack.

Divide the dough into 2 balls, and roll each ball into a circle around 2.5cm/1" larger than your pie plate.

Place one pastry circle into the base of the pie plate. Mix all the filling ingredients together in a bowl, then tip this into the pie plate.

Place the remaining dough circle over filling, trim any excess pastry, and pinch the edges of the dough circles together

Cut slits in a cross shape, in the middle of the top crust, for steam to escape.

Bake for 10-15 min. Then lower oven to 165C/ 325 and bake for a further 35-45 minutes.

BANANA BREAD

Ingredients

240g/ 9 oz plain/ all-purpose flour
225g/ 8 oz mashed bananas
150g/ 5 oz chopped nuts*
80ml/ 3 fl oz vegetable oil
120ml/ 4 fl oz water
3 medium eggs
1 tsp vanilla essence
1 tsp baking soda
2 tsp baking powder
1 tsp cinnamon
½ tsp nutmeg

Method

Preheat the oven to 170C / 325F / Gas Mark 3

Beat together the mashed banana, oil, eggs and water until creamy and not too lumpy.

Add the flour, baking soda, baking powder, vanilla essence and spices.

Beat well and stir in the nuts, if using nuts. Spoon batter into a greased or lined loaf pan, spreading the batter evenly.

Bake for around 45-55 minutes or until a knife inserted comes out clean. Allow to cool completely before slicing. Delicious served spread with butter!

Nuts are optional and can be excluded.

ZUCCHINI BREAD

Ingredients

120g/ 4 oz plain/ all-purpose flour
60g/ 2½ oz finely ground almonds
175g/ 6 oz grated courgette/ zucchini
1 mashed ripe banana
6 tbsp butter, soft
60g/ 2 oz Greek yogurt
3 medium eggs
2 tsp cinnamon
1 tsp baking soda
¾ tsp Stevia powder
1 tsp vanilla essence
¼ tsp nutmeg
¼ tsp baking powder
Pinch salt

Method

Preheat the oven to 180C / 350F / Gas Mark 4

Mix together the butter and eggs.

Add the courgette / zucchini, banana, Stevia, vanilla, Greek yoghurt and flour, and mix on high.

Sift in the flour, cinnamon, salt, nutmeg, baking powder and baking soda and mix well until it is all completely combined in a batter.

Spoon batter into a greased or lined loaf pan, spreading evenly.

Bake for 25-35 minutes or until a knife inserted comes out clean. Allow to cool completely before slicing.

FRUIT LOAF

Ingredients

450g/ 1 lb mixed fruit
225g/ 8 oz pitted dates, chopped
75g/ 3 oz plain all-purpose flour
75g/ 3 oz wholemeal flour
25g / 1o z chopped walnuts
275ml/ 9 fl oz water, boiling
4 tbsp orange juice
3 tsp baking powder
1 tsp mixed spice

Method

Preheat the oven to 170C / 325F / Gas Mark 3

In a large bowl, add the chopped dates then pour the boiling water over them. Allow to cool completely.

When cool, mash the dates in the water before adding in all the other ingredients.

Thoroughly mix it all together until you have a pourable batter.

Spoon batter into a greased or lined loaf pan, spreading evenly.

Bake for 75 to 90 minutes, or until cake is firm to touch and a skewer comes out clean.

Leave in the tin to cool. Delicious served sliced and spread with butter!

DATE LOAF

Ingredients

240g/ 9 oz of self-raising flour
140g/ 4½ oz of pitted chopped dates
240ml/ 8 fl oz of milk
3 medium eggs
1 ripe banana, mashed
1 tsp baking soda
Handful of flaked almonds for top

Method

Preheat the oven to 180C / 350F / Gas Mark 4

Sieve the flour and baking soda into a large bowl.

Add the chopped dates and mashed banana, followed by the milk and eggs.

Mix well together until all is combined.

Pour batter into a greased or lined loaf pan, spreading evenly.

Sprinkle the top with flaked almonds, if desired.

Place in oven for 45 minutes, or until cake is firm to touch and a skewer comes out clean.

Allow cake to cool before serving.

GRANOLA BARS

Ingredients

450g/ 1 lb mashed ripe banana
180g/ 6 oz rolled oats
70g/ 3 oz walnuts, chopped
70g/ 3 oz sunflower seeds
70g/3 oz dried cherries or cranberries, chopped
55g/ 2 oz sliced almonds
1 tsp vanilla essence
1 tsp cinnamon
¼ tsp rock salt

Method

Preheat the oven to 180C / 350F / Gas Mark 4

In a large bowl, mash the bananas until smooth, then add the vanilla essence.

Place the rolled oats into a food processor (or blender or nutribullet) and pulse until they are coarsely chopped. Be careful not to blitz them into a powder, and add to the banana mixture in the bowl.

Roughly chop the walnuts and cherries/cranberries and add these, plus all the remaining ingredients into the banana-oat mixture until thoroughly combined.

Lightly grease a large square or rectangular baking dish (around 20cm x 30cm/ 8.5" x 12.5" is ideal) and line with a piece of greaseproof paper/ baking parchment. Spoon the mixture into the lined dish, and press down firmly.

Bake for 25-30 minutes until firm and lightly golden at the edges.

Allow to cool for 10 minutes in dish, then carefully lift out, placing on a rack to cool completely. Cut into slices once cooled. Store in an airtight container.

FLAPJACKS

Ingredients

3 mashed, ripe bananas
175g/ 6 oz chopped, pitted dates
180g/ 6 oz rolled oats
80ml/ 3 fl oz vegetable oil
1 tsp vanilla essence

Method

Preheat the oven to 180C / 350F / Gas Mark 4

Mash the bananas in a large bowl, then add the dates, oil and vanilla essence and mix together thoroughly.

Stir in the oats and leave for 5 minutes, so that the oats absorb the wet mixture and oil.

Lightly grease a large square or rectangular baking dish (around 20cm x 30cm/ 8.5" x 12.5" is ideal) and line with a piece of grease-proof paper/ baking parchment. Spoon the mixture into the lined dish and press down firmly.

Bake for 25-30 minutes until firm and lightly golden at the edges.

Allow to cool for 10 minutes in dish, then carefully lift out, placing on a cooling rack to cool completely. Cut into slices once cooled.

PANCAKES

Ingredients

120g/ 4 oz plain/ all-purpose flour
240ml/ 8 fl oz milk
3 egg yolks
3 egg whites
1 tbsp baking powder
Blueberries, handful (optional)

Method

In a medium bowl, sieve together the flour and baking powder, then stir in the milk and egg yolks and beat until smooth.

In a large mixing bowl, beat the egg whites until stiff peaks form. Fold the whipped egg whites into the batter until all combined.

Heat a lightly oiled griddle or frying pan over medium heat.

Pour or scoop the batter onto the griddle, in whatever size of pancake you prefer.

When you see bubbles start to form and pop, it should be time to flip your pancake over. Cook the other side until it is also golden brown.

Serve hot, and if you wish to add some sweetness, try fresh strawberries, raspberries or blueberries and/ or a tiny drizzle of honey.

You could also use homemade applesauce either in the pancake mix or on top!

PECAN CRUST PUMPKIN PIE

Ingredients

Pecan Crust:

300g/ 10 oz pecans
6 large dates, pitted
2 tsp cinnamon
1 tsp vanilla essence
3 tbsp water
Pinch salt

Pumpkin Filling:

425g/ 15 oz canned pumpkin
1 x 350g/ 12 oz can coconut milk
5 large dates, pitted
150g/ 5 oz whole pecans for top
3 medium eggs
1 tsp cinnamon
½ tsp ground ginger
¼ tsp nutmeg

Method

Preheat the oven to 190C / 375F / Gas Mark 5

Make 'pecan meal' for the crust by finely grinding the 300g / 10 oz pecans in a food processor or nutribullet.

Next, blend the dates in a food processor until smooth. Add these to the rest of the crust ingredients and combine until well-mixed.

Lightly grease a 23cm/ 9" pie pan and press ONLY ¾ of this mixture evenly to the bottom and sides. Keep ¼ of this crust mixture back for the crunchy topping.

Bake for 10-15 minutes or until browned. Set aside. To make the filling, blend the coconut milk with the five chopped dates until completely smooth, then combine the pumpkin, eggs, milk, and spices and beat until smooth.

Pour the pumpkin mix into the crust and bake, uncovered for 25 minutes.

Then sprinkle the remaining crust mix, plus the pecans, over the top and return to the oven for another 25 minutes until topping is golden and crunchy but not burned.

CHRISTMAS FRUIT LOAF

Ingredients

450g/ 1 lb mixed dried fruit
100g/ 4 oz glace cherries/ candied cherries
175g/ 6 oz plain/ all-purpose flour
225g/ 8 oz dates, chopped
300ml/ 10 fl oz water
3 tsp baking powder
2 tsp mixed spice
4 tbsp orange juice
Zest of 1 orange

Method

Preheat the oven to 170C / 325F / Gas Mark 3

Grease a 900g/ 2lb loaf tin and line with grease-proof paper/ baking parchment.

In a large bowl, add the chopped dates then pour boiling water over them. Allow to sit in the water and cool completely. When cool, mash the dates in the water.

Add everything else to the dates and water, and mix well.

Bake for around 90 minutes, checking regularly after 60 minutes. If the top is browning too quickly, before the middle is cooked, cover with parchment. Test with a sharp knife in the middle, when it comes out clean the cake is cooked.

Allow to cool in tin, then decorate as desired.

CHRISTMAS COOKIES

Ingredients

150g/ 5 oz plain/ all-purpose flour
200g/7 oz cashew butter (or nut butter)
4 medium eggs, lightly beaten
2½ tsp vanilla essence
1½ tsp Stevia powder, plus extra to dust
2 tsp mixed spice
1 tsp cinnamon
¼ tsp baking powder
Pinch of salt

Method

Preheat the oven to 170C / 325F / Gas Mark 3

In a large bowl, mix together the flour, baking powder, Stevia, spices and salt.

Mix your nut butter with the eggs and vanilla essence until smooth.

Add to the dry ingredients and mix well to form a dough. If your dough is too dry, add a little milk or water.

Line a baking tray / cookie sheet with baking parchment/ greaseproof paper.

Roll the dough onto a floured surface, or onto baking parchment, then cut out cookies – using Christmas cookie cutters if you have them – and place onto tray.

Bake for around 20-25 minutes or until nicely golden.

Allow to cool completely, then dust with extra Stevia if desired.

COCONUT TRUFFLES

Ingredients

100g/ 4 oz cream cheese
3 tbsp dessicated/ shredded coconut
2 tbsp coconut oil
3 tbsp coconut cream
Juice of 1 lemon
1 tsp Stevia powder

Coating:
¼ cup dessicated/ shredded coconut

Method

Blend the cream cheese and coconut oil in a mixer, until smooth. Add the coconut cream, salt, lemon juice and Stevia and blend further.

Stir in the 3 tbsp of shredded coconut and mix through with your hands. Cool in fridge for 30 minutes to allow mixture to firm up.

Now roll mixture into small balls, coating each ball in shredded coconut. Keep in fridge in a sealed container.

CHOCOLATE TRUFFLES

Ingredients

200g/ 8 oz unsweetened chocolate
100g/ 3½ fl oz double / heavy cream
150g/ 6 oz cocoa powder

Method

To make the ganache truffle centre, chop up your chocolate finely and set aside. In a medium saucepan, heat the cream gently, but do not allow to boil. Remove from the heat and add the chopped chocolate so that it is covered by the cream completely.

Allow chocolate to melt in the hot cream, then stir well and whisk until smooth. Place in the refrigerator to firm up – around 30 minutes.

Remove and roll into small balls, then roll each ball in cocoa powder.

Keep in fridge in a sealed container.

For a sweeter taste, you can add artificial sweeteners to your ganache.

Or even try orange oil, mint essence or vanilla essence for different flavourings.

CHOCOLATE MOUSSE

Ingredients

450g/ 1 lb pitted dates, chopped
800ml/ 1¼ pint coconut milk
10 tbsps cocoa powder
6 drops vanilla essence

Method

Chop your softened dates finely and to your blender or food processor, with 2 rounded tbsps of coconut milk. Blend on high until dates are blitzed.

Add the remaining coconut milk and the cocoa powder and blend together until smooth, then lastly add the vanilla essence.

Divide the mousse between 4 dishes and refrigerate for at least 2 hours before serving.

Delicious served with fresh berries and / or whipped cream.

RICE PUDDING

Ingredients

170g/ 6 oz pudding or risotto rice
30g/ 1o z butter
150ml/ 5 fl oz full fat/ whole milk
1 tsp cinnamon or cocoa (optional)

Method

Preheat the oven to 150C / 300F / Gas Mark 2

Take a large dish and butter the inside, then melt the rest of your butter in a saucepan, over a low heat.

Add the rice and milk to the pan and mix well. (For a richer version you can use cream instead of milk).

Pour the mixture into your pudding dish, and place in the middle shelf of the oven.

Cook for around 60 minutes, or until rice is soft and fluffy.

Serve with a sprinkle of cinnamon or cocoa powder. Also delicious with a swirl of berry compote or sugar free jam.

COCONUT MACAROONS

Ingredients

400g/ 14 oz dessicated/ shredded coconut
400ml/ 14 oz condensed milk
1 large egg white
1 tsp pure vanilla essence
¼ tsp almond extract
Pinch of salt

Method

Preheat the oven to 170C / 325F / Gas Mark 3

Line a baking sheet with greaseproof paper / baking parchment and set aside.

Whisk your egg white until light and fluffy.

In a large bowl combine the shredded coconut, condensed milk, salt, vanilla, almond extract and the whipped egg white.

Using a spatula, fold carefully until all the ingredients are combined.

Drop a tablespoon at a time of the mixture on a baking sheet, spaced apart.

Bake for about 15-20 minutes, or until golden brown.

Allow to cool before serving.

CHOC NUT FUDGE

Ingredients

3 cups semi-sweet chocolate chips
400ml/ 14 oz condensed milk
¾ cup chopped nuts
1 ½ tsps vanilla extract
Pinch of salt

Method

In large saucepan, melt the chocolate chips, condensed milk and salt over a low heat until all melted together.

Remove from the heat then stir in the vanilla essence and chopped nuts.

Line a shallow square or rectangular pan with greaseproof paper / baking parchment, and pour in the mix, spreading evenly.

Place in the refrigerator for at least 2 hours or until firm.

When set, cut into squares, and store in a sealed tub in the refrigerator.

CHOCOLATE FUDGE SAUCE

Ingredients

125 ml/ 4 fl oz milk (or almond/ cashew milk)
50g/ 2 oz pitted dates, chopped
3 tbsp cocoa powder

Method

Put dates and milk into a blender or food processor and blend together until smooth.

Pour this into a saucepan and bring to the boil. Lower the heat to a simmer, and continue to stir over a low heat for 5-10 minutes, until it starts to thicken.

Remove from the heat and stir in the cocoa powder, mixing well until it is fully blended in.

Store in a sealed glass jar and eat cold, or re-heat in a pan to a pouring consistency as needed.

CHOCOLATE BUTTERCREAM

Ingredients

140g/ 5 oz mashed sweet potato
85g/ 3 oz pitted dates, chopped
30g/ 1 0 z cocoa powder
3 tbsp coconut oil
2 tbsp nutbutter of choice
125ml/ 4 fl oz milk (or almond/ cashew milk)
1 tsp vanilla essence

Method

Cook your sweet potato in its skin, in the oven, for 30-40 minutes. Allow to cool, then scoop out the flesh and mash. Discard the skin.

In a saucepan, melt the coconut oil and whisk in the cocoa powder to create a smooth chocolate syrup.

In a food processor, blend together the milk and chopped dates and blitz until smooth. Next, add the mashed sweet potato, nut butter, and vanilla essence and blend until smooth.

Add all this to the chocolate syrup and mix well until smooth.

Use your buttercream right away or keep in fridge until later use. If you wish to pipe it, remove from fridge to allow to soften for an hour before using.

VANILLA CREAM CHEESE FROSTING

Ingredients

340g/ 12 oz cream cheese
4 tbsp double/ heavy cream
1 tsp vanilla essence

Method

In a large bowl, add the cream cheese and vanilla essence and mix well. A hand-held or stand mixer works well for this recipe.

Add one tablespoon of heavy cream at a time and continue to mix until a smooth consistency appears.

Use your frosting right away or keep in fridge until later use. If you wish to pipe it, remove from fridge to allow to soften for an hour before using.

STRAWBERRY POPS

Ingredients

250g/ 9 oz ripe strawberries
100ml/ 4fl oz un-sweetened apple juice
1 tsp honey

Method

Whizz the strawberries, apple juice and honey in a blender.

Divide between 4 lolly moulds and freeze for at least 5 hours or until set.

You can also add chopped strawberries – or other fruit – into each mould.

For a creamier pop, replace the apple juice with natural yoghurt.

AGAVE CARAMEL SAUCE

Ingredients

3 tbsps butter
¾ cup Agave syrup
¼ cup double/ heavy cream
Pinch of salt

Method

Melt the butter in a saucepan over a medium heat.

Add the agave syrup, followed by the cream and pinch of salt.

Cook over a medium heat, stirring constantly as it starts to caramelise and thicken. This should take around 10 minutes.

Remove from heat and store in a sealed glass jar in the refrigerator.

Allow to reach room temperature before pouring over desserts.

RECIPES ♥ TUTORIALS

Cake & Bake ACADEMY
Est. 2014

RESOURCES ♥ INSPIRATION

The Only Cake & Bake Recipes You'll Ever Need!

A great new series of essential baking books containing the best ever selection of recipes!

RECIPES ♥ TUTORIALS   RESOURCES ♥ INSPIRATION

Printed in Great Britain
by Amazon